# SPECIALTY CUISINE
# COOKBOOK,
## By Mama Denise

Special Edition – Golden Nugget Exclusive –
Selected Specialty Recipes from Mama Denise©

## Mama Denise

**author**HOUSE®

*AuthorHouse™*
*1663 Liberty Drive*
*Bloomington, IN 47403*
*www.authorhouse.com*
*Phone: 833-262-8899*

*Published by AuthorHouse  02/26/2021*

*ISBN: 978-1-6655-1828-4 (sc)*
*ISBN: 978-1-6655-1826-0 (hc)*
*ISBN: 978-1-6655-1827-7 (e)*

*Library of Congress Control Number: 2021903908*

*Print information available on the last page.*

*Any people depicted in stock imagery provided by Getty Images are models, and such images are being used for illustrative purposes only. Certain stock imagery © Getty Images.*

*This book is printed on acid-free paper.*

*Because of the dynamic nature of the Internet, any web addresses or links contained in this book may have changed since publication and may no longer be valid. The views expressed in this work are solely those of the author and do not necessarily reflect the views of the publisher, and the publisher hereby disclaims any responsibility for them.*

# CONTENTS

# DEDICATION

*To All Those Who Understand the Love of Cooking and Love to Cook.*

# MISSION STATEMENT

*One spoonful of Mama Denise's heavenly delicious meals or desserts and your tastebuds will thank you over and over again and you will want more and more and more!!!*

# PREFACE

Thank you for your investment in purchasing Mama Denise's Specialty Cuisine Cookbook. These dishes are not inclusive. These are some of my favorite ones which I am sure you will enjoy cooking, eating, and sharing with others.

The wonderful thing about cooking is that for your prepared dishes to come out exactly the way you want them to – you must enjoy cooking; I would even go as far as to say, "You must love to cook".

Even though cooking can be therapeutic; I suggest not to cook while you are angry or distracted. Cooking requires your undivided attention. Prepare your food with love.

One of my greatest feelings of achievement for each dish I have prepared is watching how my family, friends and customers enjoy them.

I did not know until I was grown that my ethnicity has a lot to do with me wanting to see people enjoy what they eat. My grandfather was from Sicily. My grandmother was an African American. Just like my recipes I have a mixture of a southern cuisine flare that is second to none. I create as I cook and so can you. I am thankful for someone suggesting to me that I write a cookbook. Keep in mind, most of the time I do not prepare my meals the same way twice. Therefore, writing this book will help me a lot.

I believe one of the secrets to my youthful look and health is that I do not eat pork or beef. I have not for over twenty years. I added a beef recipe in this book as a compliment for those of you who like to eat beef. Please note I did not stop eating pork or beef for religious reasons at all. It was just something I felt lead to do many years ago, and it is working for me.

If you are a good cook you will know how to take these recipes and add them to the meat of your choice.

Here are some added tips:

- It is important to understand what seasonings go with the proper dish or you will end up with a disaster. Leave the kitchen to those who know what they are doing. Give this book as a gift to someone else – if you do not like to cook.
- Work in a clean kitchen and clean your kitchen as you go – both tips came from my mother who was not always the best cook, yet she could clean a house like no one I have ever known to this day.
- Make sure your meats and vegetable are fresh. Try not to refreeze your meats after defrosting. This not a good practice. You do not want to end up making your customers, family, or friends sick at the stomach after eating your prepared meals.
- When making any type of desserts do not use the same utensils. Keep your utensils for vegetables, meats and desserts separate. Make sure your utensils have been thoroughly cleaned prior to use each time.
- Do not prepare your meats, vegetables, or desserts at the same central location (area) in your kitchen. Keep them separate from one another. You do not want an onion and pepper smell in your cake mixture.
- Always, always cook with love. Have the ones you are always preparing the meal for in mind. Eating is universal and it is a way of communicating your love to each one for whom you are preparing a meal.
- Most of my recipes will feed 4 – 6 people. Double, triple or cut in half according to your desired amount.
- I use "Calphalon" pans (I received them as a gift, and I prefer this brand) for most of my cooked dishes (I am not being paid to advertise for them as of this publishing – maybe once their sales go up because of my cookbook - they will!!!
- Cakes and Pies are typically good for serving sizes of 6-8 depending on how big you cut your slices. Eggs and Milk

should always be Room Temperature and not cold. This works better for the perfection of mixing the dry ingredients with the wet ingredients.

- Butter/Margarine for the pie can be cold – cut in cubes to place on top of the apple/pear ingredients before putting the top crust on top.
- I use the stove/oven for all my cooking. Cooking times will vary depending on whether you are using a gas oven or electric oven. If the recipe calls for, 350° that will be fine if using a gas oven. Follow the recipe for cakes and pies for 45 minutes cooking time. If using an electric oven, change the oven temperature to 355° which still may require the same cooking time. It depends on your appliance. Keep an eye on your cakes and pies. A cake is done when you can stick a toothpick in the middle and it comes out clean.
- Cakes are cooked in 9.1.5" cake pans. You will need 2 of these pans for layer cakes.

Pies pans are your basic size 9". I suggest you purchase the pie crust that is in a roll. It comes with two pie crust. You would simply unroll them and shape according to the size of the pan. You can cut off any edges that may fall over the edges of the pan. I use the back of a spoon or a fork pressing on the edges to seal the top and the bottom to give them their appearance.

- Calories are not included in this Cookbook – they can be easily found through Google. You may want to purchase a cooking thermometer for your Fried Chicken. I cook by eye and taste. If you have any questions, please visit our website which is included at the end of this book.
- Use tongs to flip the chicken a few times as it browns evenly, and then…if it looks done, it must be done right? Wrong. Too-hot oil will make for a dark exterior while the inside's still raw. That is gross. Combat this issue with a meat thermometer (not the one you may use for your oil!)

Do not be afraid to break the chicken's crust to take the meat's internal temperature; it should read 165 degrees. A little trick I teach is take a knife and stick it in your chicken just a little that helps to make sure it is done too. Plan on the whole process taking around 15-18 minutes, keeping in mind that white meat will cook faster than dark. Also, majorly important: Crowding the pan or deep fryer with chicken will lower the oil's temperature. This will up the cooking time and make the breading greasy.

Enjoy these dishes as I have over the years with family, friends, customers, and co-workers.

Bon Appetit

Written in Love,

*Mama Denise*

# SMOTHERED CHICKEN

8 Skinless, Boneless Thin or Medium Cut Chicken Breast

(Feeds 4-6)

Use a skillet or deep-dish frying pan (preferably cast iron)

## Ingredients

- Slap your Mama Seasoning (SYMS) (I always cross out the word "Slap" with a black marker). As of right now they are not paying me to endorse them. Once their sales go us – maybe they will then. Nevertheless, this is my favorite seasoning on mostly every dish I prepare. I cannot give you the true essence of my recipes without it. Except for cakes and pies, of course!
- garlic powder (approximately 1 tablespoon)
- 1 medium onion (White) (Finely chopped) or 1 brunch of green onion (Finely Chopped)
- 1/2 Green Pepper (finely chopped)
- 1/2 Red Pepper (finely chopped)
- 2 fresh Garlic Cloves (added once juices are noticeable in the pan)
- 3 tablespoons of Canola Oil (or your choice of cooking oil)
- 1 – 12-ounce Jar of Chicken Gravy
- Add Lots of Love

- 1 teaspoon of Gravy Master
- 1 teaspoon of Soy Sauce
- 1 teaspoon of Crushed Peppers (Optional)

Sauté your onions, and peppers separately in the Canola Oil – Seasoned with SYMS and Garlic Powder, Garlic Cloves - FYI: your choice of oil – may taste different from Mama Denise's though… May need to season it to your taste with a little more of the SYMS, and Garlic Powder the amounts.

Once done, (cook for 3-5 minutes) remove from the pan do not clean out the pan. You need those seasonings for your meat.

Season your Chicken Breast with SYMS, Garlic Power, Chopped Parsley (fresh or seasoning) on both sides and if you desire another seasoning be creative, but not too creative –

Put a lid on your pan and place it on low and let the chicken begin to make its own sauce drippings. Cook for about 20-30 minutes on low – Checking on your pot frequently, making sure it does not cook too fast or dry out. Your chicken will make its own juices if you follow these instructions correctly.

Once you are sure the Chicken is done – you will know because it will be so ever tender. Take the onions and pepper mixture and add it back into the pan spreading it around by a teaspoon on top of each piece of chicken. Cover again and let it simmer on low for about another 5 minutes. Then add your gravy mixture and with a tablespoon of Hot Sauce. Let it simmer for about another 10 minutes. You will have to season to your desired taste. If you like spicy you can add some Cayenne Pepper seasonings to your taste. I do not always measure my seasoning. That one is on you.

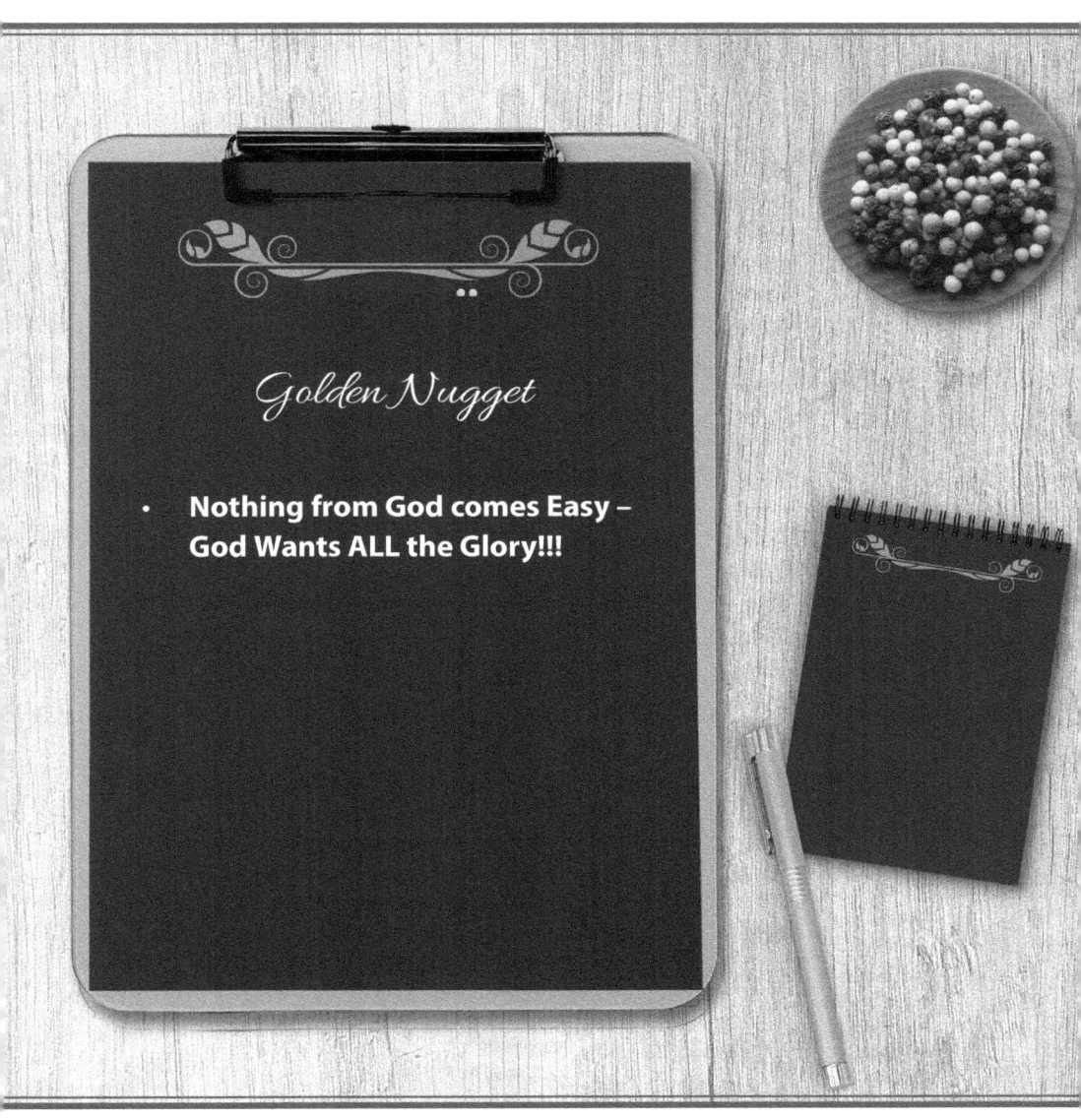

*Golden Nugget*

- **Nothing from God comes Easy –
  God Wants ALL the Glory!!!**

# SAUTÉ KALE

This is my all-time favorite vegetable. I could eat Kale every single day. For this recipe you can use frozen (quick chopped steam) Kale or fresh Kale (my preference is frozen Kale – you can substitute Chopped Spinach if you do not like Kale both are healthy and nutritious with this recipe. You will find out in my recipes I always use Onions and Peppers (the white onions make a huge difference in the taste of my recipes – I discovered that a few years ago) If you want to use yellow onions do not blame me if it does not take as good as Mama Denise's!

Can use a skillet or deep-dish cooking pan (cast iron pan preferably)

- 2 Packages of Frozen Steamed Chopped Kale (you can use Fresh Kale – Kale contains a lot of water. Therefore, it will shrink to a lesser amount, so make sure you buy enough to accommodate your desired servings)
- 1 Medium White Onion (Finely Chopped)
- 1 Small Red Onion (Finely Chopped)
- 1 Small Green Pepper (you can also add red peppers, yellow peppers & orange peppers and (1) small Jalapeno Pepper (take out all the seeds if you do not want your Kale too spicy) these will add to the taste and your dish will be beautifully colored as well) (Finely Chopped)
- 3 bottle caps full of Canola Oil (or your choice of cooking oil) medium heat

Sauté your onions, and peppers as we did in our other recipe seasoned them with SYMS and garlic

- 1 tablespoon of minced garlic or 2 fresh garlic cloves sliced
- 1 teaspoon of Garlic Powder
- 1 teaspoon of Cilantro
- 1 tablespoon of Margarine or Butter
- 1 pinch of Light Brown Sugar

Once your onions and peppers have caramelized move them to the left side of the pan open your frozen Kale packages – Make sure your heat is on low – the water from the Kale and the oil in the pan may cause a little splash of steam (you do not need to steam the Kale first) or add your freshly chopped Kale to the right side of the pan gently combining both ingredients with a large cooking spoon (preferably with holes in it) over a medium/low temperature.

Add the Margarine or Butter to the mixture and stir it again evenly

Add a little bit more of SYMS (you do not want the Kale to be too salty)

Add your "pinch" of light brown sugar to the mixture and stir it again evenly

Add two more Tablespoons of oil (make sure you have plenty of liquid in the pan. Kale is full of water should make its own liquid) (plus if frozen you should have some extra liquid)

Add another sprinkle of SYMS and Garlic Powder

You want to taste it with a teaspoon to make sure it is your desired taste (please do not use that same spoon again – wash it!! No double dipping!

Put your heat on Simmer/Low for about 5 – 10 minutes. Checking on the contents that it is cooking properly and not drying out. If you must add a teaspoon of water or another 1/2 teaspoon of oil – stirring consistently that the ingredients have mixed well

Serve with an additional side – White Rice, Brown Rice or Mama Denise's Home Fried Sweet Potatoes, Fresh Corn on the Cob, Frozen Steamed Corn or just eat them alone – they are Heavenly Delicious!

~~~~~~~~~~~~~~~~~~~~~~~~~~~~~~~~~~~~~~~~~~~~~~~~~~~

Golden Nugget

- **All You Need is LOVE**

# HOME FRIED SWEET POTATOES

6 Medium size Sweet Potatoes or Yams

(*If you can find the Sweet Potatoes/Yam Steam bag even better. Follow the instructions below once done*)

Boiled until done make sure you cool them enough to peel off the skin. Cut your Sweet Potatoes in small or medium size cubes and keep them to the side until ready to add to your mixture

- 1 medium onion (white) (finely chopped)
  1/2 cup of a green pepper (finely chopped)
  1/4 cup of a Red Pepper (finely chopped)
- 3 fresh garlic cloves (added once juices are noticeable in the pan)
- 1 green onion (finely chopped) Optional
- 1/4 cup shallot
- 2 tablespoons of Canola Oil (or your choice of cooking oil)
- SYMS (Season to Taste)
- garlic powder (approximately 1 tablespoon)
- Black Pepper (if you and your guest are spicy) (1/4 teaspoon)

Sauté your onions and peppers and leave them in the pan. Once they are caramelizing on a low heat, add your sweet potatoes mix well for a few minutes.

They should be gone in less than 2 minutes – Enjoy! Serve as a Breakfast side with Mama Denise's Scrambled Eggs, Cheese Omelet, Bacon, Sausage (turkey sausage, turkey bacon or your favorite)

~~~~~~~~~~~~~~~~~~~~~~~~~~~~~~~~~~~~~~~~~~~~~~~~~

*Golden Nugget*

- **Life can be Heavenly Delicious When You Have All the Right Ingredients**

# DEEP FRIED TILAPIA
# OR FRIED SHRIMP

This recipe can be used with any Seafood Dish. I use it with my Shrimp as well as Catfish and any other type of seafood dish when frying

5-6 Fresh or Defrost Tilapia, Fish or 30 Large Shrimp (deveined, tail off and peeled) If you want to do the work – you can buy with tail on and take off yourself

1 cup of yellow corn meal
1/2 cup of flour
1 1/2 tablespoons of SYMS
1 tablespoon of garlic powder
1 teaspoon black pepper
1 medium size bowl or a new brown paper bag (sandwich size for this recipe)

Add these ingredients in the bowl or Brown Paper Bag – Mix well

(You can also substitute a Fish Seasoning like *Louisiana New Orleans Style Fish Fry* over the counter instead of the Corn Meal and Flour mixture – make sure to add about 4 tablespoons of corn meal to that seasoning unless you like salty) My opinion – no pun intended

2 cups of Canola oil (or your desired cooking oil) Oil need to be extremely hot or your fish will fall apart. (Do not burn your oil)

Cook until Golden Brown

Serve with your desired side – French Fries are always the best with this dish

~~~~~~~~~~~~~~~~~~~~~~~~~~~~~~~~~~~~~~~~~~~~~~~~~~~~~~~~~~

## Golden Nugget

- **God Allowed It! He Does ALL Things well! There are no Mistakes in the Kingdom of God**

# TURKEY MEATLOAF

2 pounds of Ground Turkey Meat
1 tablespoon of SYMS (or seasoned to taste)
1 teaspoon garlic powder
1/4 cup of Italian seasoned Breadcrumbs
1/4 cup of green peppers – finely diced
1/4 cup of white onion – finely diced
1/4 cup of red pepper – finely diced
8-ounce can of tomato paste
2 tablespoons of tomato dice green pepper sauce (optional)
1/4 cup of Ketchup
1/4 cup Sweet Baby Ray Barbecue Sauce (Original)
1 egg

Mix all your ingredients together with the 2 pounds of Ground Turkey Meat (Make sure everything is mixed well) You can improvise with the seasoning (add jalapeno (with or without the seeds – removing the seeds taste most of the heat out of your meal if you do not like too spicy)

Shape and put in a loaf pan on 355 (Electric Stove) 350 (Gas Stove) bake for about 45 minutes to an hour

10 minutes before done you can pour about a tablespoon of ketchup across the top of your meatloaf

Your meatloaf is going to be so tender and mouthwatering ready for you and your guest

~~~~~~~~~~~~~~~~~~~~~~~~~~~~~~~~~~~~~~~~~~~~~~~~~~~

**Golden Nugget**

- **Successful People are Always Leaving Clues!!! #payattention**

# CALIFORNIA BURGER
## Mama Denise Style

2 pounds of Ground Turkey or Beef
Fresh Hard Rolls (4)
Finely chopped green onion (Scallions) – 1/3 cup
Finely chopped green Pepper – 1/3 cup
1 teaspoon of SYMS
1 teaspoon of garlic Powder
1/4 cup of canola Oil
Finely chopped medium jalapeno pepper(optional)

Mix all ingredients together – prepare your skillet with 1/8 of a cup of oil (or you desire) thumb print in the middle of the burger once placed in the pan – Shape your patties into 4 equal parts. Right before placing your burger in your skillet; put a thumb print in the middle of it for even cooking.

Prepare your Roll (your choice) Options: add Mayonnaise, Tomatoes, Lettuce, extra white Onions (optional), Mustard (optional), ketchup enjoy

~~~~~~~~~~~~~~~~~~~~~~~~~~~~~~~~~~~~~~~~~~~~~~~

## Golden Nugget

- No one can live healthy off one meal a week; Sunday should not be the only day you feed your soul.

# DEEP FRIED CHICKEN WINGS
## With or Without Mama
## Denise's Special Sauce

1 brown medium paper bag
1 cup of white flour
1/4 cup of corn meal

Or instead, you can buy - Louisiana Crispy Fried Chicken Seasoning Mix – and add 1/4 cup of White Flour – if you like salty – leave it just like it is without adding any flour – Use a Deep Fryer or a Skillet – Make sure you have enough oil in the pan to cover 3/4 of the chicken

1 Tablespoon SYMS
1 teaspoon garlic powder
Canola Oil
Himalaya Pink Salt

Make sure your chicken is cleaned by removing any feathers left on your Chicken Wings (do not rinse with water or place in water)

Combine all ingredients in your brown bag, add 3 to 4 chicken wings at a time and shake – if you are serving for a larger audience use a larger bag and increase chicken wings put into the brown bag "Shake" making sure chicken is evenly covered

Place them into the hot oil – (From Cooking Tip) Use tongs to flip the chicken a few times as it browns evenly, and then…if it looks done, it must be done right? Wrong. Too-hot oil will make for a dark exterior while the inside's still raw. That is gross. Combat this issue with a meat thermometer (not the one you may use for your oil!) Do not be afraid to break the chicken's crust to take the meat's internal temperature; it should read 165 degrees. A little trick I teach is take a knife and stick it in your chicken just a little that helps to make sure it is done too. Plan on the whole process taking around 15-18 minutes, keeping in mind that white meat will cook faster than dark. Also, majorly important: Crowding the pan or deep fryer with chicken will lower the oil's temperature. This will up the cooking time and make the breading greasy. Sprinkle while hot with Himalaya Pink Salt- Serve Immediately – Pour Mama Denise's Special Sauce over the top (Optional)

*Golden Nugget*

- **Honesty is a Key Element in Living a Prosperous Life**

# BEEF POT ROAST

Angus Beef Chuck Steak – 0.93 – 1.55 lbs.
(can substitute Stew Meat, Boneless Chuck Roast or Chuck Tender Roast)
3 White Potatoes
3 Sweet Potatoes
1 medium White Onion
1 medium Green Pepper
1 medium Yellow Pepper
1 medium Orange Pepper
1 small Jalapeno (optional) (if do not want too spicy take the seeds out)
1 leek
3 fresh Garlic Cloves
SYMS to taste (approximately 1 tablespoon or more)
1 tablespoon of Garlic Powder
1/2 teaspoon Black Pepper (optional)
1 1/2 tablespoon of Canola oil
1 teaspoon Parsley or Fresh Parsley (1/2 cup)
1 tablespoon Worchester Sauce
1 teaspoon Soy Sauce
1 teaspoon Gravy Master
1/2 cup of Spring Water

(Use a Slow Cooker put on high or if making on the stove using a regular cast iron deep pan that has a cover – cook on medium heat – then low last 10 minutes)

Season your meat with SYMS, Garlic Powder, Black Pepper – brown in a cast iron or pan applicable with Canola oil – do not cook all the way through – just cook long enough on both sides for the seasoning to get into the meat. Take out if using a Slow Cooker and place inside the Cooker. Make sure to wash your potatoes – slice them, leave the skin on them and place on top of the Steak/Roast. Slice and add your Onion, Garlic Cloves, Green Peppers, Orange Peppers, Yellow Peppers, slice Leek onto the top of the meat. Add your liquid ingredients. Put on high (slow cooker) and cook for about 2 1/2 - 3 hours. Watch periodically to make sure there is enough liquid in the pan. If cooking on top of the stove – should cook about 30-40 minutes – medium to low heat

You will know when it is ready to eat – the meat will become very tender. Enjoy!

(If cooking on top of the stove - follow the same instructions above – have your heat on low until everything is added so the meat does not cook too fast – the slower the meat cooks – the more tender it will be!!!!) Once all ingredients have been added cook on medium high with a cover – watch periodically to make sure there is enough liquid in the pan.

## Golden Nugget

- You will make mistakes in
  life that is inevitable
  Learn from them –
  Do NOT Repeat Them

# HOME MADE HONEY CORN BREAD

5 Tablespoons of salted butter (Melted) (save 1 Tablespoon) or Country Crock
5 Tablespoons of unsalted butter (Melted) (save 1 Tablespoon) or Country Crock
1 cup of all-purpose Flour
1 cup of yellow corn meal
¾ cup of sugar (1 cup if you want sweeter)
1 1/2 teaspoons baking powder
1/2 teaspoon of baking soda
1/2 teaspoon of salt
1 cup of buttermilk, regular milk, or skim milk
2 teaspoons of honey (put one teaspoon on the side for the topping) (optional)

Preheat oven to 350 (Gas Stove) 355 (Electric Stove) -

Oil your pan with Canola oil and dust flour it – please make sure excess flour is removed. You can also use a stainless-steel cooking (stickless) pan and spread with Pam Canola Spray – Set aside

Whisk together your dry ingredients first – separately mix your wet ingredients together – once well mixed – make sure you make like a "well" in the middle of your dry ingredients – pour your wet ingredients in the middle well of the dry ingredients and mix everything together

Pour the batter into the prepared pan – (you can use a 9 1.5" cake pan, or an oblong/square cake pan. Have not tried it yet – but an iron cast skillet pan will work too) bake until golden brown – not dark brown) You can also use the old fashion method of sticking a clean toothpick in the middle of the corn bread and it comes out clean. If it does your Corn Bread is ready… Take your remaining Honey and the butter mix spread over the top of the Corn Bread – Option: can add Cinnamon Sugar instead of honey to your butter mix to pour over the top or just leave plain. Serve hot/immediately

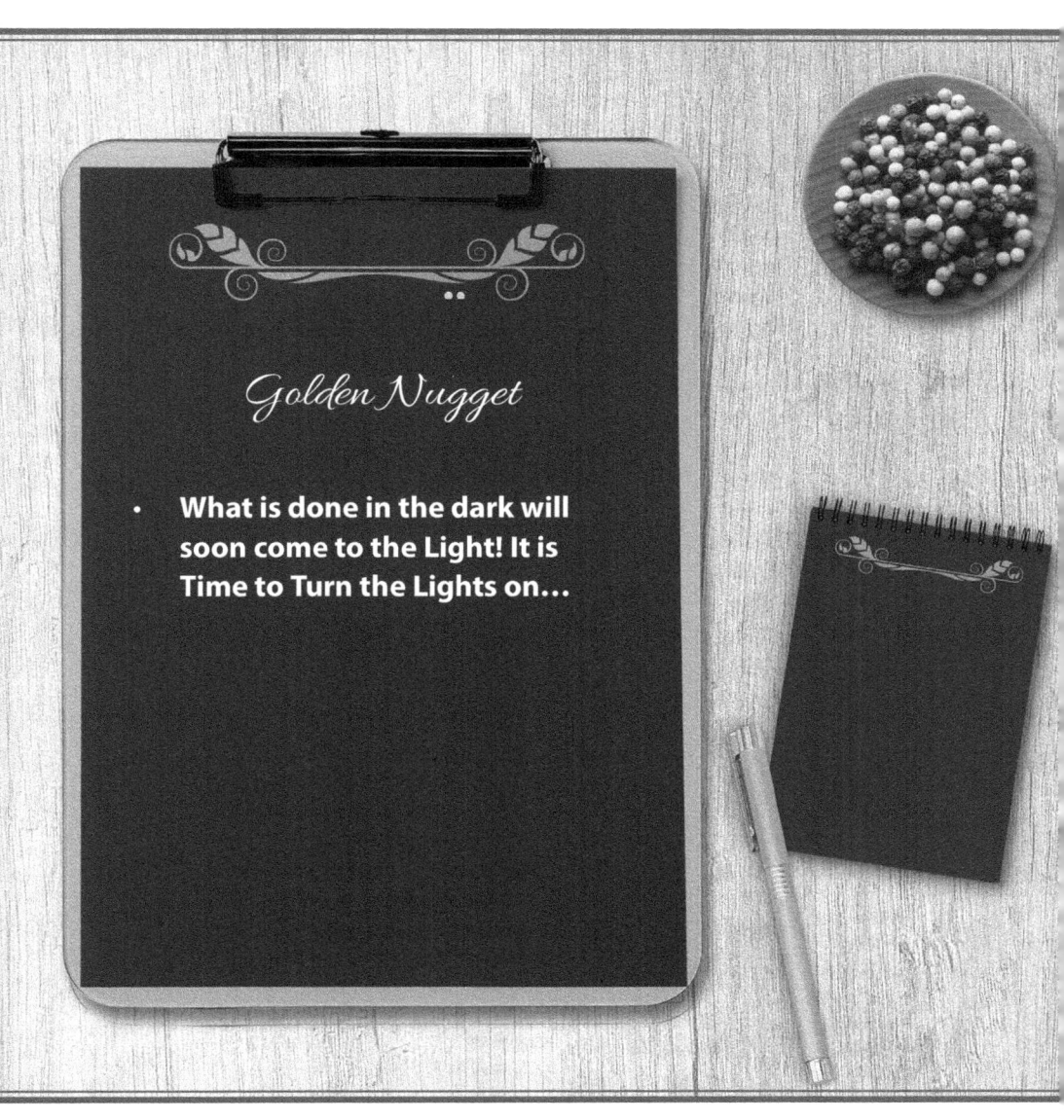

*Golden Nugget*

- **What is done in the dark will soon come to the Light! It is Time to Turn the Lights on…**

# SHRIMP WONTON

- 20 Wonton Wraps
- Package of X-Large or Jumbo Shrimp
  Peeled, deveined
- 1 egg white (Beaten)

Deep Fryer or Pan to fry Wonton in preferably Canola Oil (or your favorite Cooking Oil. I cannot promise you they will taste as good as mine, if you use a different type of oil

Utensil Brush to spread the Egg White slightly beaten onto the four corners of the Wonton Wraps

Boil your shrimp for about 2 – 3 Minutes until they turn Pink

Put in a bowl, add SYMS, Garlic Powder, and Old Bay Seasoning to taste

(set aside)

Take your brush dip it into the bowl and lightly spread the Egg White on all four corners (not a lot – enough to be used as glue to seal the wontons) fold into a triangle shape

Take one seasoned shrimp put in the middle of the Wonton Wrap and seal in a triangle shape. Make sure it is completely closed. If the shrimp is too large for the wonton – cut a little off and save a couple of those pieces to combine in another Wonton Wrap

Make sure your oil is hot but not smokey – if the oil is too hot your Shrimp Wontons will come out darker than they should – they should appear lightly crispy (crunchy but not burnt) You need to watch so they do not get too dark. Turn over so both sides are the same color (they will float on the top of the oil) Remove and set to the side – Repeat until all your Shrimp Wontons are cook.

Serve Immediately

Can brush with some melted butter or margarine for added taste – sprinkle a little bit of Old Bay on the top of the Wontons while they are piping hot… Enjoy!

## Golden Nugget

- **FAITH! Period**
  **#queenoffaith**

# SHRIMP EGG ROLLS

Egg Roll Wraps (Can find in most stores in the refrigerator section)
Package of X-Large or Jumbo Shrimp Peeled, deveined (15-25 per bag)
Salad Mix (your choice)
Beaten Egg White (1 or 2 – depending on how many Egg Rolls)
1 teaspoon of SYMS (Season to taste after you have boiled your shrimp for 3-4 minutes)
1 teaspoon garlic powder
1/2 tablespoons seafood seasoning (Old Bay)

Boil the Shrimp first for about 3-4 minutes until lightly pink. Get your Deep Fryer or Pan to fry Wonton in preferably Canola Oil - or your favorite Cooking Oil. I cannot promise you they will taste as good as mine, if you use a different type of oil

Utensil Brush to spread the Egg White slightly beaten onto the four corners of the Wonton Wraps

Mix the Shrimp into your salad mix (after seasoning them) Evenly put in the mixture to be able to roll the wraps (triangle wise. to come into the shape like a regular egg roll tube. Drop in the deep fryer or frying pan for about 1 to 2 minutes. You must watch them they will brown quickly when the grease is hot.

Now if you want to be creative you can add whatever vegetables you want, mushrooms, bean sprouts (must be completed drained), cabbage, shredded carrots…

You need to serve the Egg Rolls immediately while they are hot. If have leftovers refrigerator – cannot promise they will still be crispy the next day – but once heated in the Microwave they will still taste just as good.

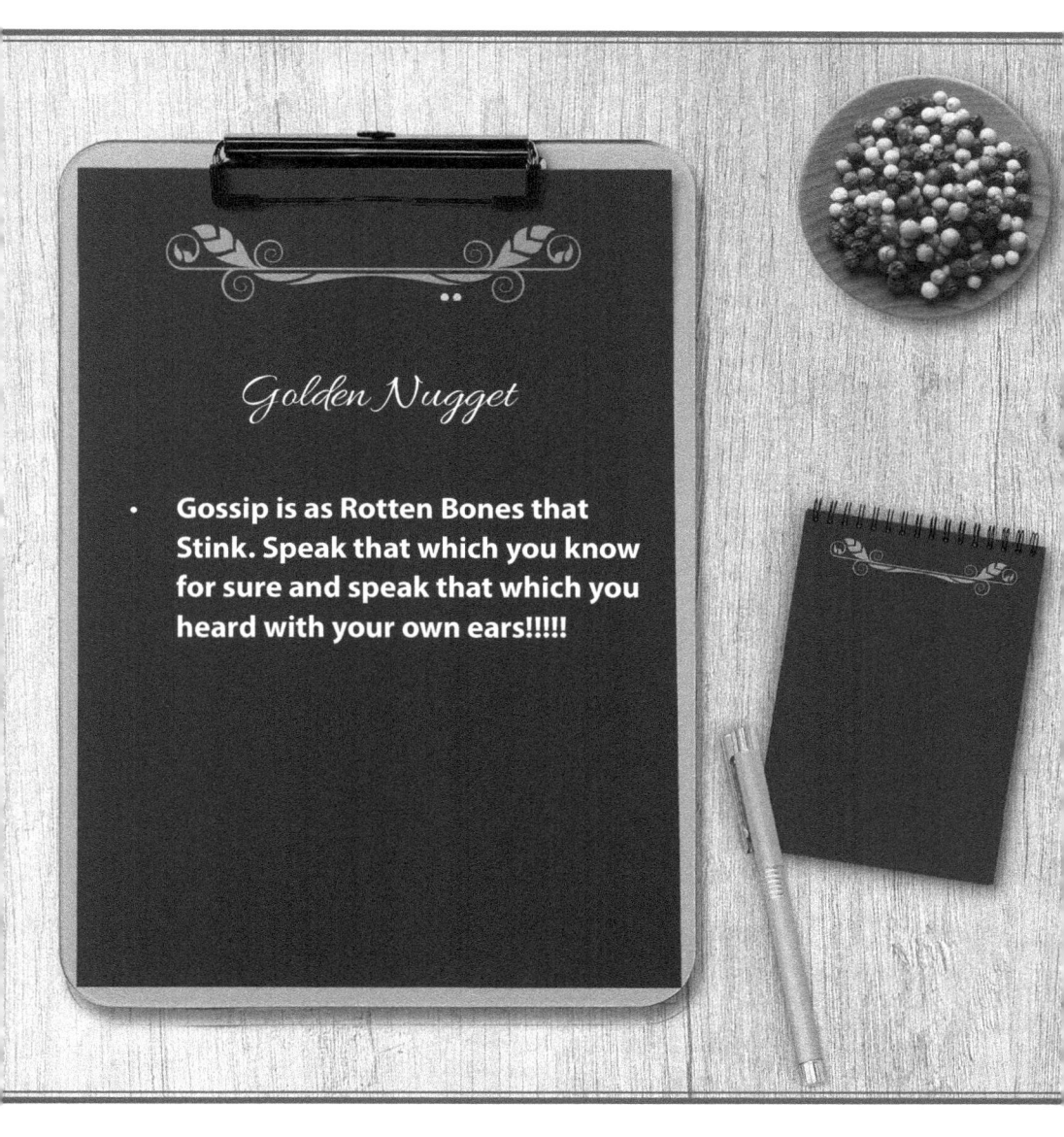

## Golden Nugget

- **Gossip is as Rotten Bones that Stink. Speak that which you know for sure and speak that which you heard with your own ears!!!!!**

# KALE CHEESE EGG OMELET

- 5 Eggs (Beaten)
- Cheddar Cheese or Mexican Mixed – 4 to 8 oz.
- Cooked Kale (see recipe in cookbook)
  Can substitute cooked Collard Greens or Spinach
- Salt & Pepper
- 1/4 Green Pepper (chopped)
- 1/4 White Onion (chopped)

Sauté your onions and peppers – of course a little bit of SYMS & Garlic (Yes, I like Garlic in just about everything that garlic can go in – that is a part of my Italian descent! Once sauté (soft and cooked – not burnt) put your onions and peppers to the side. (take out of pan)

Scrambled your eggs, add a pinch of milk (or a teaspoon of pancake mix – if you are making pancakes with this meal – share a teaspoon of pancake mix to add to your scrambled eggs. This will help fluff up your eggs.

Add – 1 tablespoon of canola oil, margarine, butter, to your pan or your favorite cooking spray

Warm your skillet or the pan you are making your omelet in. Do not make the pan too hot your eggs will burn. Once your pan is hot enough "pour" your eggs into the pan once the bottom is cooked flip it over – turn off the heat on your pan but leave the pan on the stove. Add your sauté onions and peppers, kale, and cheese (up to the amount your desire) fold it close over. Press it down so all the ingredients come together. Cut down the middle to serve two or give the entire Omelet to one person if they think they can handle it. Bon Appetit

*Golden Nugget*

- **Parents: Never Make the Mistake to Compare your Child(ren) with one another or anyone else for that matter. Even if they are the same gender. God has uniquely designed and created each one of us according to our individual characters and personality.**
**#evenidentificaltwinshavedifferentfingerprints**

# BARBECUE TURKEY WINGS

- Large Roasting Pan
- 6 Turkey Wings
- SYMS
- Garlic Powder
- Paprika
- Parsley Flakes or Fresh Parsley
- Good Seasoning Italian Dressing
- 2 Large Carrots
- 1 Large White Onion
- 3 Garlic Cloves
- 1 Large Green Pepper
- Canola Oil
- Good Seasons Italian Dressing
- 3- medium red potatoes
- 1 cup of water (Spring Water, if possible)

Line your large *Roasting Pan* with Aluminum Foil brush bottom of the pan with some Canola Oil

Cut up all your side ingredients sliced or cube size (your preference) and put to the side.

Place your Turkey Wings in the Pan Season with SYMS, Garlic Powder, Black Pepper, Paprika on both sides – Take your Good Seasons Italian Dressing and pour approximately a cap full over each Turkey Wing on one side only as you did with the Chicken Thighs in the previous recipe. One full cupful of Canola oil on top of your Turkey Wings. Pour one cup of water directly around the bottom of the pan without pouring it onto the Turkey Wings. After about an hour of cooking – Spread your Vegetables over the top of the Turkey Wings Evenly. Sprinkle some SYMS, Garlic Powder, Black Pepper and Paprika over the vegetables.

Put a cover on your Turkey Wings and do not open the pan up for at least 1 1/2 hours (adding the water is particularly important so your pan does not dry out and it will create steam to help tenderize the Turkey Wings. Cook on 350° (Gas Oven) 355° (Electric Oven)

Check the Turkey Wings after 1 1/2 hours to see if they are cooking properly take some of the juices from the bottom of the pan and drizzle over top of each wing. Add more water, if necessary – your pan should not be dry out.

Stick a fork in one of the Turkey Wings to see if they are tender. Cook about another 35 minutes – the last 15 minutes take the top off the pan and allow the Turkey Wings to brown. You will know when they are done – because they will be smelling so good and practically falling off the bone.

When serving – carefully remove them from the pan to place on your serving dish.

Serve with Corn Bread Stuffing, White or Brown Rice, Sweet Peas, Collard Greens or Seasoned String Beans or of course Mama Denise's Favorite Kale Recipe*

*Golden Nugget*

- **Do Not Hang with Angry People
You Will Become Angry Too!**

# SPICY CHICKEN THIGHS

- 6 Skinless, Boneless Chicken Thighs
- Good Seasons Italian Dressing Packet (*Follow directions*) (Good Seasoning Italian Seasoning Glass Bottle)
- SYMS
- garlic Powder
- black Pepper (Can replace with Cayenne Peppers if you like hot/hot)
- Canola Oil

Set your Oven on "Broil"

Season your Chicken thighs on both sides with SYMS, Garlic Power, and a little Black Pepper. Prepare the Good Seasons Dressing as directed. Shake the bottle once you have added the ingredients accordingly. Drop about a tablespoon over the top of the chicken thighs - make sure they are covered but not soak with the Italian dressing. Just put on the top of the Chicken thighs. Take one cap full of canola oil (or your favorite oil – as I like to say cannot guarantee it will taste as good as Mama Denise's if you use different ingredients and pour over top of the Chicken thighs.

Place into the oven (Broil) Set your Timer for 20 minutes (make sure to watch the thighs depending on the oven they may cook fast – turn over once as they are browning. Cook to your desired but not too long or they will no longer be tender. You do not want them rubbery.

Serve as they are or with some Homemade Mash Potatoes and Steamed Asparagus – Heavenly Delicious

You can add my Special Sauce to the top of the chicken thighs during the last 5 minutes (See Recipe)

*Golden Nugget*

- **Faith gets God's Attention and Draws Him to You!**

# MAMA DENISE'S SPECIAL SAUCE

- 1 cup - Sweet Baby Ray Barbecue Sauce "Original" -
- 1/4 cup -Hot Sauce
- 1 tsp – Butter (Unsalted/Salted) or Margarine
- 1 tsp – Honey
- 1 tsp - Crush Red Peppers – Optional

Mix all ingredients together with a spoon and drizzle over your *"Spicy Chicken Thighs" or "Fried Chicken", "French Fries" or "Deep Fried Fish"*

*Golden Nugget*

- **God Always Gives Us More than What We Ask!!!!**

# MAMA DENISE'S COLE SLAW DRESSING

8 oz bag Angel Hair Cole Slaw

- 1 cup of Mayonnaise
- 4 tablespoons White Sugar
- 3 tablespoons of Lemon Juice or Juice from a Fresh Lemon
- 2 tablespoons of White Vinegar
- 1 teaspoon of Ground Black Pepper
- 1/2 teaspoon of Salt
- 1 teaspoon of Celery Seeds (Seasoning)

Mix all ingredients together – Stirring well and pour over your Cole Slaw. Make sure to toss the Cole Slaw several times that all the dressing is mixed evenly.

This dressing can be used on sandwiches and wraps too instead of plain mayonnaise. Heavenly Delicious! Enjoy!!!

*Golden Nugget*

- **God Cannot Give You Clearance for Landing when You are Not Sure of Your Destination.**

# CHUNKY CHICKEN CHILI
## Cook in Slow Cooker

2 Large Chicken Breast with the Rib (Remove the skin)
4 medium Chicken Thighs (Preferably skinless/boneless) If only have Chicken thighs with skin and the bone (remove all the skin)
Season Meat with SYMS, Garlic Powder, Black Pepper
2 packs of Chili Seasoning
1 small green pepper
1 medium white onion
1 teaspoon of minced garlic
1 medium jalapeno pepper (if prefer mild – remove the seeds)
1 Large beefsteak tomato
1 Can 16 oz of Pinto Beans
2 Cans - Green Chives and Tomatoes (1- 8 oz/ 1 – 16 oz)
1 Can 16 oz - Tomato Sauce
1/4 Cup of Canola Oil

Place 1/4 cup in the bottom of your Slow Cooker (turn on high) Place your Chicken in the bottom of the pan

Combine all liquid ingredients including the Pinto Beans in a separate bowl – season with SYMS, Garlic Powder, Black Pepper and Minced Garlic – Stir the mixture – Add Chili Seasoning (McCormick or your favorite brand of Chili Seasonings) to the mixture making sure it is mixed well – Pour the liquid over top of the Chicken

Mixing well without breaking up the chicken in the bottom.

Sliced (do not dice or cube them) your Green Pepper, White Onion, Jalapeno pepper and Beefsteak tomato lay them across the top of the liquid mixture and place your top on the pot.

Cook for 8-9 hours. (Check after a couple of hours, the Vegetable topping should have cooked to the point you can stir them into the liquid mixture. Depending on how fast your Slow Cooker cooks you will know when your Chunky Chicken Chili is done when the meat is in pieces and you can visibly see the chicken has mixed itself with the Chili mixture. Kind of chopped the chicken up with a large spoon to your desire.

Enjoy with Mama Denise's Cornbread, Cheese Crackers, Regular Crackers or Homemade Bread.

## Golden Nugget

- **Do not Hate on People who are Blessed and Being Blessed. They are Decreeing and Declaring "Open Your Mouth and say Something Too"**

# BROWN STEW CHICKEN

(6) Skinless Boneless, Chicken Thighs
*Louisiana New Orleans Style Chicken Seasonings*
¼ cup of all-purpose flour
1 teaspoon of SYMS
1 small clean/new brown paper bag
¼ cup of Canola Oil (enough to cover the bottom of your pan)
1/2 cup of white Onion (sliced or diced)
1/2 cup of green Peppers (sliced or diced)
1/2 cup of yellow peppers (sliced or diced)
1/2 cup of red peppers (sliced or diced)
1 small plum tomato (sliced)
1/2 cup of orange peppers (optional)
¼ cup of Soy Sauce
1 tablespoon of Kitchen Aid Gravy Mix
¼ cup of Worchester Sauce

Slice up your vegetable ingredient (not the tomato into the hot pan with canola oil)

Sauté those vegetables – sprinkle SYMS on top of the vegetables remove from the pan and put in a separate small bowl to the side – do not clean your pan out – let the seasoning from SYMS and the vegetable remain in the oil (low heat)

Put your seasoning Chicken Fry Seasoning in the brown paper bag – add the ¼ cup of White All-Purpose flour in the bag and shake it up making sure both ingredients are mixed well.

Heat your cooking pan to medium hot and place your chicken thighs three (3) at a time in the brown (sandwich size) paper bag and shake – place in the hot oil – repeat with the other three (3) chicken thighs and place in pan together making sure they are browning (not dark/not burnt) turn them over. Once brown – turn your heat down to low – add the sauté vegetables on top of the brown meat – cover your pan for about 5 minutes and let the meat get tender.

Mix your 3 sauces together (Soy Sauce, Worchester Sauce, and Gravy) pour over top of your Chicken Thigh – slice your tomato and top on top of the vegetables already in the pan (onion, green peppers etc.) sprinkle a little bit more of SYMS and Garlic Power over top. Cover and place on low heat for about 10-15 minutes watching it closely. Your liquid cannot leave the pan. As a matter of fact, it should be making more liquid coming from the chicken. You will know when the meat is done because the thighs will be so tender, they will begin to come apart.

You can improvise with Chicken Breast – I would not suggest Chicken legs (but if you got a gut feeling this will work – go for it) Make sure to make enough because it is going to go fast.

Serve over top of White or Brown Rice, Mash Potatoes, or the other sides I suggest in this Cookbook. Heavenly Delicious. Enjoy!!!

## Golden Nugget

- **When God Gives Us Instructions, we "Must" do them "EXACTLY" the way He says. "EXACTLY" is the definitive word. If you do not do this – do not expect to receive what He has promised!!!**

# MAMA DENISE'S
# MASHED POTATOES

6 medium size white potatoes
2 sticks of salted or unsalted butter or margarine
1/2 tablespoon of Salt
1/4 teaspoon of Pepper
1/2 cup of Skim Milk (or Whole Milk)

(Boiled and peeled your Potatoes once done) Quick way to cook potatoes (wash them well, coat with butter or margarine) poke four holes in the top of your potatoes (use a fork) place in your microwave select the cook potato setting (put in 6) and let cook until Microwave lets you know they are ready – Some Microwaves will only let you cook 3 at a time – if necessary, do this… You can start mixing all ingredients while the last 3 are cooking and just add them once they are done.

Let cool for a few seconds – so you will not burn your hand - remove the skin

Place in a bowl – immediately put in 1 stick of butter (while still hot) and 1/2 cup of milk mash with a hand masher. Then use a hand beater until smooth - you may have to add more milk and butter until the potatoes are smooth and creamy

Taste a spoonful making sure it is perfect (do not double dip your spoon – wash your teaspoon. Add additional salt or pepper if needed - Sprinkle with Parsley or your favorite cheese prior to serving. Serve Hot - Immediately

*Golden Nugget*

- **Do Not Get Discouraged in Prayer. Keep Praying – Prayer Works!!!**

# MAMA DENISE'S PEACH CHEESECAKE

**Crust**
1 ¼ cups Graham Crackers (I buy the whole Graham Crackers and break them up myself into crumbs)
1 stick of (Salted or Unsalted) Butter, softened or melted
3 tablespoons of your choice of white granulated sugar

**Filing**
1 Cup peeled and sliced peaches divided (for the puree) Can use can or fresh peaches
¾ cup white granulated sugar of your choice
3 8 oz packages Cream Cheese
2 large eggs
1/2 teaspoon vanilla extract
1/4 Sour Cream
2 tablespoons – all Purpose Flour

**Glazed Peach Topping**
1/2 cup white granulated sugar
2 teaspoons of cornstarch (may need a little bit more)
1/4 cup Water
1 1/2 cups of peeled and sliced peaches (for decoration on top)
1/2 teaspoon Lemon Juice

Spring Cake Pan (especially for Cheesecakes) Preheat oven to 350°F Lightly spray an 8-inch springform pan with nonstick cooking spray.

Combine in a medium bowl graham cracker crumbs, butter, and sugar; stir to moisten crumbs. Press crust into bottom and slightly up sides of springform pan (I prefer just the bottom with the crust – this is your choice if you want to put the crust on the sides too).

Bake in the center of the oven for 6 minutes (watch closely as not to cook too long and burn the crust) until the crumbs just begin to brown. Remove from the oven; cool. Leave oven on.

## Filing

Puree peaches in mini food processor (if you do not have a food processor you can use your regular cake mixer – slow your roll – so you do not make a mess set aside)

In the mixer bowl, beat cream cheese on a medium speed; then, gradually add sugar and beat until smooth. Add eggs, one at a time; beat until light and whipped. Beat in vanilla, sour cream, and pureed peaches; then, stir in flour. Pour mixture into prepared crumb crust.

Wrap the bottom and sides of the springform pan in foil and set the pan on a baking sheet with sides. Set the baking sheet on the middle rack of the oven, pour one half inch of hot water onto the baking sheet; then, carefully push the rack in and close the oven door. (Watch that the water does not elaborate – add more if needed in the bottom of the pan)

Bake for 10 minutes then reduce oven temperature to 325F. Bake for one hour or until set. Cheesecake is done when a knife inserted in center comes out clean. The cake should still jiggle a bit when moved. Remove from the oven and from the water bath and cool 45 minutes to one hour. Cover and chill until ready to serve.

## Glazed Peach Topping

Whisk sugar, cornstarch, and water together in a saucepan over medium heat and bring to a boil. Fold in reserved peach puree and peach slices, bring mixture back to boil, stirring constantly; then, reduce heat and simmer 1 to 2 minutes or until sauce is thickened and translucent. Do not overcook the peaches. Stir in lemon juice, remove from heat, and cool. Chill until ready to serve.

To serve, arrange cooked peaches decoratively over top of cheesecake, allowing sauce to drip down the sides.

Options: Fresh, Frozen, can peaches, packed in juice or water can be used successfully for this recipe. I have tried with Strawberries and Cherries. Our favorite topping though is Peaches. Enjoy! Be Creative

## Golden Nugget

- **Gratefulness opens the door for more things to be Grateful for...**

# VANILLA CAKE WITH WHITE & BLACK ICING

3 cups Cake Flour
1 tablespoon Baking Powder
1/2 teaspoon Salt
1/4 teaspoon baking soda
1 1/2 cups butter, softened
1 ¼ cups sugar
4 eggs
2/3 cup milk (can substitute with Skim Milk)
1 1/2 teaspoons Vanilla Extract

Heat Oven to 350° (Gas Stove) 355° (Electric Oven) Coat 3 (9 inch) cake pans with no-stick cooking spray (or brush with Canola Oil bottom and sides evenly – take a ¼ cup of flour and shake pan hitting on the sides and bottom until the entire cake pan is covered. Set aside.

Mix all the dry ingredients making sure they are mixed well with a spoon. In a separate bowl combine all the wet ingredients and beat on medium speed. Mix the dry and wet ingredients together beat until well mixed. Divide evenly in prepared pans.

Bake 19-23 minutes or until toothpick inserted in center comes out clean. Cool 10 minutes. Remove from pans to wire rack to cool completely.

*Using a shortcut for Icing this cake*

Purchase a Can of Vanilla Icing and a Container of Milk Chocolate Icing (Mix the icing in the cans well once complete – spread one side of the cake with the Vanilla Icing and the opposite side with Chocolate Icing – Put multicolored sprinkles on top of the cake. Let the Icing sit for about 10 minutes in the refrigerator – then remove and put in a cake holder with cover (refrigeration is optional) Cake is good for one week fresh outside of the refrigerator

*Golden Nugget*

- **Being Confident is not conceit!
Keep Doing You!!!!!**

# APPLE/PEAR PIE

2 – 9" Pie Crust (shells) (Pillsbury) in box (Refrigerator Section)
2 – 9" Pie Pans (or buy the Pie Crust already made in the Pan)
(If you already know how to make Pie Crust from scratch – go for it - make it use your favorite recipe)
3 – Apple Crisp (Medium to Large) or Fuji Apples
(Peel and slice the apples in cube triangle)
2 teaspoons of Cinnamon (can add a little more, if desired)
2 teaspoons of Nutmeg (can add a little more, if desired)
1 teaspoon of All Purpose Flour
1 stick of salted or unsalted butter
1 pinch of salt
1/2 cup of White granulated Sugar
1/2 cup of Light Brown Sugar

Follow the directions on the Pie Crust box, if needed

Mix all your ingredients in a large bowl. Put in apples first, then add your cinnamon, nutmeg, 1 pinch of salt, Sugars – on the bottom of the pie pan put about 4 cubes of the slice butter, once all your ingredients are mixed in the bowl add the mixture to the pie shell, Top with the remaining butter cut in cubes – sprinkle on top of the butter about a teaspoon of light brown sugar

Cover the top with the extra crust – pinch the sides. Put 3 slits in the top of the Pie Crust. Place foil loosely around the edges before putting in the oven.

Bake at 375° Gas Oven (380°) Electric Oven for 20-25 minutes.

Remove foil and bake until crust is golden brown, and filling is bubbly, 20-25 minutes (Cooking time will vary – keep your eye on the pie – through the glass door window – try not to open (unless necessary) when we open the oven, we change the temperature. When golden brown – remove from the oven and let cool on a wire rack or another cool surface (that will not burn from the heat of the pan) of place on a clean dish towel or cookie sheet to cool.

Serve Warm, if possible, with Vanilla or Butter Pecan Ice Cream

Golden Nugget

- **God has the Final say!**

# MAMA DENISE'S CARROT CAKE

2 cups all Purpose Flour
2 teaspoons Baking Soda
1/2 teaspoon Salt
2 teaspoons ground cinnamon
3 large eggs
2 cups sugar
3/4 cup Canola Oil
3/4 cup Buttermilk (Whole or Skim Milk)
2 teaspoons Vanilla Extract
2 cups Grated Carrot
1 (8 ounce) can crush pineapple, drained
1 (3 1/2 ounce) can flaked coconut
1 cup chopped pecans or walnuts

***You can add raisins to this recipe if you like***

**Buttermilk Glaze** (See below)
**Cream Cheese Frosting** (See below)

Line 3 (9 inch) round cake pans with wax paper; lightly grease and flour wax paper set pans aside

Stir together flour, baking powder, salt, and cinnamon (set aside)

Separate bowl beat eggs and add sugar, oil, milk, pure vanilla extract. Make sure everything is mixed well

Add in Carrots, Pineapples and Coconut – Add the Dry Ingredients and mix well

(medium speed) Pull into the cake pans

Bake at 350° (Gas Oven) or 355° (Electric Oven) 25-30 minutes or until a wooden pick inserted into the center comes out clean. (I prefer to let the cake cool long enough to get it out of the pan put on the main plate or dish you want to use and then Drizzle the half of the Buttermilk Drizzle evenly over layers; cool in pans on wire racks 15 minutes. (Do not put too much Glaze the cake may fall apart if you apply too much Glaze the cake may be too moist) Save the remaining Glaze to use when serving to your guest or right before you take the personal slice.

Spread Cream Cheese Frosting between layers and on top and sides of cake.

Buttermilk Glaze
1 Cup of Sugar
1/2 Cup Butter or Margarine
1/2 Cup Buttermilk
1 Tablespoon Light Corn Syrup
1 teaspoon Vanilla Extract

Bring all ingredients to a boil in a small saucepan, and cool for 3 minutes.

Cream Cheese Frosting
¾ Cup Butter or Margarine
1 (8 ounce) Package Cream Cheese, softened
1 (3 ounce) Package Cream Cheese, softened

3 Cups Sifted Powdered Sugar
1 1/2 Teaspoons Vanilla Extract

Beat butter and cream cheese at medium speed with electric mixer until creamy. Add powdered sugar and vanilla; beat until smooth. Spread on the cake. Can top with chopped pecans or walnuts.

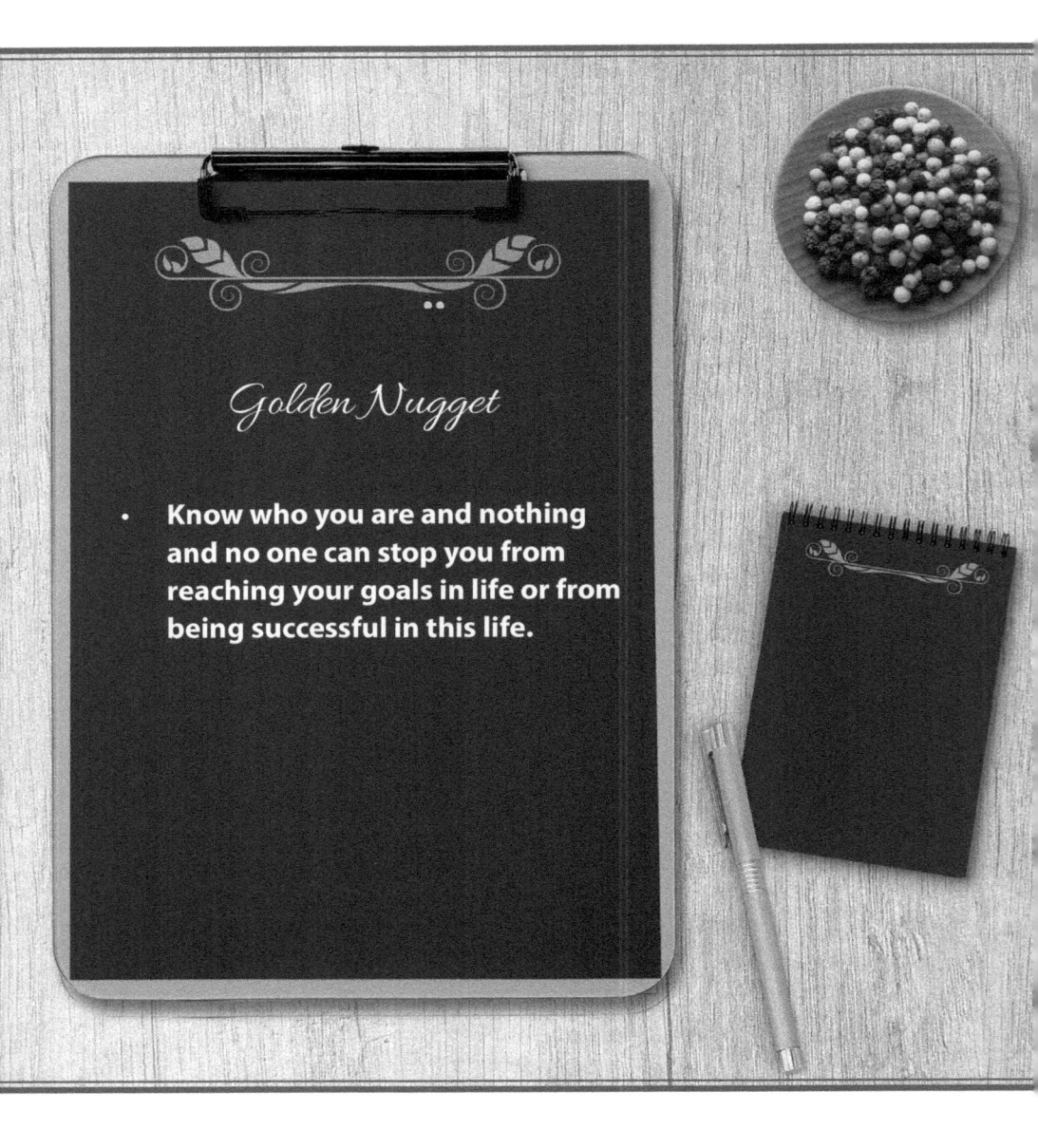

## Golden Nugget

- Know who you are and nothing
  and no one can stop you from
  reaching your goals in life or from
  being successful in this life.

# PEPPERMINT COCONUT CAKE
## *Shortcut Version*

Betty Crocker White Moist Cake Mix – Follow the Directions
Instead use 3 Whole Eggs (including yoke) instead of 3 Egg Whites
1 Box of Instant French Vanilla Pudding Mix
1 (regular tablespoon – not measuring spoon) Sour Cream
Can use Whole Milk or Fat Free Milk
16-ounce Sweetened Coconut Flakes
1 Crushed Candy Cane or Crushed Starlite Peppermints (2)
2 – 9 1.5" Cake pans – Greased and flour (or Spray with Cooking Spray/bottom and sides)

I prefer to manually grease my cake pans and add about a tablespoon of flour and rocking the sides and shaking until the whole pan is coated with flour

Please follow these directions clearly so you do not end up with a Pudding Cake

Use two different bowls – One for wet ingredients and one for dry ingredients

Combine all your dry ingredients and stir for about 2-3 minutes making sure the Instant Pudding is mixed completely throughout the Cake Mix (especially important)

Combine all your wet ingredients from the box instructions. Mix about 1 minute with an electric mixer. Add the wet ingredients to the dry ingredients **Add the Sour Cream in a few minutes after you have combined all ingredients and the Beater is in motion.**

Beat the ingredients for about 2 minutes or until all ingredients are mixed well.

Pour into to the 2 separate cake pans - Bake according to the instructions on the Cake box

While your cake is cooking - While Cake is cooking - Take your Peppermint (crushed with your rolling pin – or clean cooking small hammer (leave the candy cane in the plastic while chopping – open on a separate plate)

Take out and cool cake before icing

Vanilla Icing

3 Cups Powdered Sugar
1/3 Cup Butter, Softened
1 1/2 teaspoon Vanilla
1 to 2 Tablespoons of Milk

In medium bowl, mix powdered sugar and butter with spoon or electric mixer on low speed. Stir in Vanilla and 1 Tablespoon of the milk

Gradually beat in just enough remaining milk to make frosting smooth and spreadable. If frosting is too thick, beat in more milk, a few drops at a time. If frosting becomes to think, beat in a small amount of powdered sugar. Frosts 13/x9 cake generously or fills and frosts an 8-9 inch two-layer cake.

or

**Shortcut**- Purchase a can of Rich & Creamy Vanilla Icing (16 Oz)

Take 2 tablespoons of Coconut Flakes and combine with the Vanilla Icing

Spread Icing one layer make sure there is ample in the middle. Sprinkle a little bit of coconut and chopped peppermint with a teaspoon - in the middle. You will not need the entire bag of coconut – save for your next cake. Top with the next cake layer. Put enough Coconut Flakes and remaining crushed peppermint on the top of the cake to cover it sufficiently.

Place the Cake in the refrigerator for about 30 minutes to settle. The Peppermint Candy flavor has a way of connecting with the Cake and the Icing. Enjoy!!! Heavenly Delicious

# ACKNOWLEDGEMENT

Thank you for your Purchase and your Investment!!!
This is just the Beginning of Many More Recipes
Please follow us on Social Media for more Cooking Ideas
Once you prepare these dishes, post them on your
Social Media Platforms, Facebook, Instagram, Twitter

Tag me @drdvmcallister
#mamadenisecuisinecookbook

Pictures of our dishes are posted on Social Media as well.

I would love to see yours posted too. Use
your imagination that is what I do!!!

For other Published Books, Blogs,
Inspirations and Podcast by

Dr Denise Victoria McAllister, Aka "Mama
Denise" visit our website

Dr. McAllister is also available for speaking engagements
and professional training opportunities

Visit www.successful1.net or
www.successful1.net/mamadenise

91

Lightning Source UK Ltd.
Milton Keynes UK
UKHW011931080321
380016UK00001B/163